This Daily Planner belongs to:

{Weekly Calendars}

"Anybody can code,
you just have to want to."

Adam Seebeck

{Weekly Planner}

Monday

Tuesday

Thursday

Friday

Month: ____________ **Days :** ______________

Wednesday

Notes

Sat/Sun

{Weekly Planner}

Monday

Tuesday

Thursday

Friday

Month: ____________ Days : ______________

Wednesday

Notes

Sat/Sun

{Weekly Planner}

Monday

Tuesday

Thursday

Friday

Month: ____________ **Days :** ______________

Wednesday

Notes

Sat/Sun

{Weekly Planner}

Monday

Tuesday

Thursday

Friday

Month: ____________ **Days :** ____________

Wednesday

Notes

Sat/Sun

{Weekly Planner}

Monday

Tuesday

Thursday

Friday

Month: ____________ Days : ____________

Wednesday

Notes

Sat/Sun

{Weekly Planner}

Monday

Tuesday

Thursday

Friday

Month: ______________ Days : ________________

Wednesday

Notes

Sat/Sun

{Weekly Planner}

Monday

Tuesday

Thursday

Friday

Month: __________ Days : ___________

Wednesday

Notes

Sat/Sun

{Weekly Planner}

Monday

Tuesday

Thursday

Friday

Month: ___________ **Days :** ____________

Wednesday

Notes

Sat/Sun

{Weekly Planner}

Monday

Tuesday

Thursday

Friday

Month: ____________ **Days :** ____________

Wednesday

Notes

Sat/Sun

{Weekly Planner}

Monday

Tuesday

Thursday

Friday

Month: __________ Days : ___________

Wednesday

Notes

Sat/Sun

{Weekly Planner}

Monday

Tuesday

Thursday

Friday

Month: ___________ Days : ____________

Wednesday

Notes

Sat/Sun

{Weekly Planner}

Monday

Tuesday

Thursday

Friday

Month: ___________ **Days :** ___________

Wednesday

Notes

Sat/Sun

{Weekly Planner}

Monday

Tuesday

Thursday

Friday

Month: ___________ **Days :** ___________

Wednesday

Notes

Sat/Sun

{Weekly Planner}

Monday

Tuesday

Thursday

Friday

Month: ____________ **Days :** _____________

Wednesday

Notes

Sat/Sun

{Weekly Planner}

Monday

Tuesday

Thursday

Friday

Month: ___________ Days : ____________

Wednesday

Notes

Sat/Sun

{Weekly Planner}

Monday

Tuesday

Thursday

Friday

Month: ____________ **Days :** _____________

Wednesday

Notes

Sat/Sun

{Weekly Planner}

Monday

Tuesday

Thursday

Friday

Month: __________ Days : __________

Wednesday

Notes

Sat/Sun

{Weekly Planner}

Monday

Tuesday

Thursday

Friday

Month: __________ Days : ___________

Wednesday

Notes

Sat/Sun

{Weekly Planner}

Monday

Tuesday

Thursday

Friday

Month: ____________ Days : ______________

Wednesday

Notes

Sat/Sun

{Weekly Planner}

Monday

Tuesday

Thursday

Friday

Month: __________ Days : ___________

Wednesday

Notes

Sat/Sun

{Weekly Planner}

Monday

Tuesday

Thursday

Friday

Month: __________ Days : ___________

Wednesday

Notes

Sat/Sun

{Weekly Planner}

Monday

Tuesday

Thursday

Friday

Month: __________ Days : ___________

Wednesday

Notes

Sat/Sun

{Weekly Planner}

Monday

Tuesday

Thursday

Friday

Month: ___________ Days : ____________

Wednesday

Notes

Sat/Sun

{Weekly Planner}

Monday

Tuesday

Thursday

Friday

Month: ___________ Days : ____________

Wednesday

Notes

Sat/Sun

{Weekly Planner}

Monday

Tuesday

Thursday

Friday

Month: ____________ **Days :** ______________

Wednesday

Notes

Sat/Sun

{Weekly Planner}

Monday

Tuesday

Thursday

Friday

Month: ____________ Days : ____________

Wednesday

Notes

Sat/Sun

{Weekly Planner}

Monday

Tuesday

Thursday

Friday

Month: ____________ Days : ______________

Wednesday

Notes

Sat/Sun

{Weekly Planner}

Monday

Tuesday

Thursday

Friday

Month: ___________ Days : ____________

Wednesday

Notes

Sat/Sun

{Weekly Planner}

Monday

Tuesday

Thursday

Friday

Month: ___________ Days : ____________

Wednesday

Notes

Sat/Sun

{Weekly Planner}

Monday

Tuesday

Thursday

Friday

Month: ___________ Days : ____________

Wednesday

Notes

Sat/Sun

{Weekly Planner}

Monday

Tuesday

Thursday

Friday

Month: ___________ **Days :** ____________

Wednesday

Notes

Sat/Sun

{Weekly Planner}

Monday

Tuesday

Thursday

Friday

Month: ____________ Days : _____________

Wednesday

Notes

Sat/Sun

{Weekly Planner}

Monday

Tuesday

Thursday

Friday

Month: ____________ **Days :** _____________

Wednesday

Notes

Sat/Sun

{Weekly Planner}

Monday

Tuesday

Thursday

Friday

Month: ____________ **Days :** ____________

Wednesday

Notes

Sat/Sun

{Weekly Planner}

Monday

Tuesday

Thursday

Friday

Month: ___________ Days : ____________

Wednesday

Notes

Sat/Sun

{Weekly Planner}

Monday

Tuesday

Thursday

Friday

Month: ____________ Days : ______________

Wednesday

Notes

Sat/Sun

{Weekly Planner}

Monday

Tuesday

Thursday

Friday

Month: ____________ **Days :** ______________

Wednesday

Notes

Sat/Sun

{Weekly Planner}

Monday

Tuesday

Thursday

Friday

Month: ____________ Days : ______________

Wednesday

Notes

Sat/Sun

{Weekly Planner}

Monday

Tuesday

Thursday

Friday

Month: ____________ Days : _____________

Wednesday

Notes

Sat/Sun

{Weekly Planner}

Monday

Tuesday

Thursday

Friday

Month: __________ Days : ___________

Wednesday

Notes

Sat/Sun

{Weekly Planner}

Monday

Tuesday

Thursday

Friday

Month: ___________ Days : ____________

Wednesday

Notes

Sat/Sun

{Weekly Planner}

Monday

Tuesday

Thursday

Friday

Month: __________ Days : ___________

Wednesday

Notes

Sat/Sun

{Weekly Planner}

Monday

Tuesday

Thursday

Friday

Month: ______________ Days : ______________

Wednesday

Notes

Sat/Sun

{Weekly Planner}

Monday

Tuesday

Thursday

Friday

Month: __________ Days : ___________

Wednesday

Notes

Sat/Sun

{Weekly Planner}

Monday

Tuesday

Thursday

Friday

Month: __________ Days : ___________

Wednesday

Notes

Sat/Sun

{Weekly Planner}

Monday

Tuesday

Thursday

Friday

Month: ___________ Days : ___________

Wednesday

Notes

Sat/Sun

{Weekly Planner}

Monday

Tuesday

Thursday

Friday

Month: __________ Days : __________

Wednesday

Notes

Sat/Sun

{Weekly Planner}

Monday

Tuesday

Thursday

Friday

Month: __________ Days : ___________

Wednesday

Notes

Sat/Sun

{Weekly Planner}

Monday

Tuesday

Thursday

Friday

Month: ___________ Days : ____________

Wednesday

Notes

Sat/Sun

{Weekly Planner}

Monday

Tuesday

Thursday

Friday

Month: __________ Days : ___________

Wednesday

Notes

Sat/Sun

{Weekly Planner}

Monday

Tuesday

Thursday

Friday

Month: ____________ Days : ______________

Wednesday

Notes

Sat/Sun

{Weekly Planner}

Monday

Tuesday

Thursday

Friday

Month: ____________ **Days :** ____________

Wednesday

Notes

Sat/Sun

Notes & Brainstorm

Notes & Brainstorm

Notes & Brainstorm

Notes & Brainstorm

Notes & Brainstorm

Notes & Brainstorm

Notes & Brainstorm

Notes & Brainstorm

Notes & Brainstorm

Notes & Brainstorm

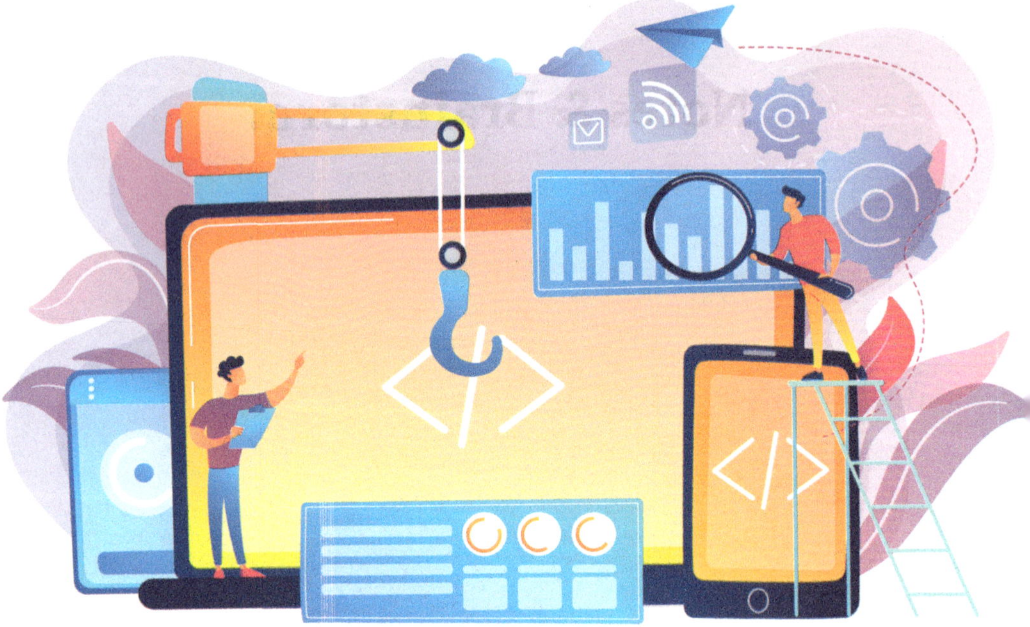

Thank You:

We hope this planner helped keep you organized and motived to code.

unQbd

Made in the USA
Monee, IL
03 November 2026

67378101R00066